THE MAJESTY OF
CAPITOL HILL

THOMAS B. GROOMS
PHOTOGRAPHS BY TAYLOR J. LEDNUM

Thomas B. Grooms

PELICAN PUBLISHING COMPANY
Gretna 2005

*The word "Pelican" and the depiction of a pelican are trademarks
of Pelican Publishing Company, Inc., and are registered in the
U.S. Patent and Trademark Office.*

Library of Congress Cataloging-in-Publication Data

Grooms, Thomas B.
  The majesty of Capitol Hill / Thomas B. Grooms ; photographs by Taylor J. Lednum.— 1st ed.
    p. cm.
  Includes bibliographical references.
  ISBN 9781589802285 (hardcover : alk. paper)
  1. Architecture—Washington (D.C.)—Guidebooks. 2. Historic buildings—Washington (D.C.)—
Guidebooks. 3. Capitol Hill (Washington, D.C.)—Buildings, structures, etc.—Guidebooks. 4.
Washington (D.C.)—Buildings, structures, etc.—Guidebooks. 5. Capitol Hill (Washington,
D.C.)—Guidebooks. 6. Washington (D.C.)—Guidebooks. I. Lednum, Taylor J. II. Title.

  NA735.W3G76 2005
  720'.9753—dc22
                                  2004017545

Printed in Singapore
Published by Pelican Publishing Company, Inc.
1000 Burmaster Street, Gretna, Louisiana 70053

To Rodger

His vision stirred me to share my love of Capitol Hill.

and

To the Capitol Hill Restoration Society

*Its leadership and commitment have given us a
community to cherish.*

Contents

Introduction

There are two Capitol Hills in Washington, D.C. They share the same geography and the same historic roots, but they are worlds apart. One is a high rise in the center of the city with an imposing building perched on the edge, its majestic white dome recognized around the world as the symbol of democracy, power, and politics—the home of the U.S. Congress. The other is a quiet, low-rise neighborhood comprised of eight thousand dwellings that fan out to the east of this famous building. These structures comprise the fourteen-block area of the Capitol Hill Historic District, the largest Victorian historic district in the country. The area is a virtual museum of nineteenth-century American architectural styles. This book is about that historic neighborhood.

For residents of "the Hill," the Capitol is merely a backdrop to their everyday lives. For them, the center of the community is a half-mile east in a one-story red brick Victorian structure with distinctive bull's eye windows and a hipped roof—the Eastern Market. "Hillites" have come here for more than a century to buy their fresh

meat, fish, and vegetables while conversing with their neighbors about events of the day—both large and small. For some, Saturday and Sunday mornings are an opportunity to indulge in the market's famous blueberry pancakes, shop at the surrounding specialty stores, and wander through the large weekend flea market.

Capitol Hill is a neighborhood that has been more than two hundred years in the making. While it has had many famous and powerful residents, including Thomas Jefferson and Abraham Lincoln, the community has been shaped largely by the middle class—artisans, craftsmen, civil servants, and merchants. George Washington and the city's French designer Maj. Peter (Pierre) L'Enfant assumed that the commercial and residential core would expand east from the Capitol and southeast to the Eastern Branch of the Potomac River (now the Anacostia River) and Navy Yard, which was established in 1799, two miles away. They envisioned a grand and fashionable eastern city built around business activity and this waterfront section of Washington. But land speculators thwarted these plans by grossly inflating the price of property around the Capitol. Furthermore by 1820 deforestation and tobacco farming in the watershed led to the silting up of the river, making it unusable for deep-draft vessels. So the city's development and fortunes turned northwest to the port of Georgetown

along the Potomac River and the area of the city between the Capitol and the White House, which by 1835 was served by the Baltimore and Ohio Railroad. As a result, Capitol Hill remained largely undeveloped until after the Civil War.

Initially, two small areas were settled in the early 1800s once the nation's capital officially moved to Washington. One was by the Capitol. Houses near the building were occupied primarily by the English, Scottish, and American (white and black) builders, artisans, and craftsmen who worked on constructing the grand edifice, which was begun in 1793. The other group of residents clustered around the Navy Yard and nearby Marine Barracks. Small frame buildings, brick boarding houses and taverns, and a couple of mansions linked the two settlements by muddy unpaved roads and were the beginnings of historic Capitol Hill. By 1814 when the British invaded Washington and burned the Capitol, White House, and other public buildings, the Hill boasted a modest community that included an outdoor market, churches, hotels, taverns, and even cemeteries. It also had another ethnic group, as Italians had been brought to Washington by President Jefferson to play in the Marine Band.

New construction after the war gave the neighborhood a more settled look in the 1820s. By 1826, after more than three decades,

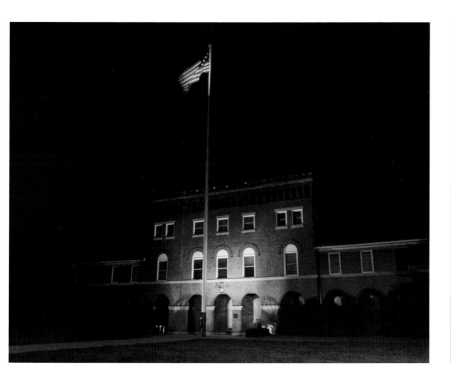

the Capitol, with its wood and copper sheathed dome by Charles Bulfinch, was finally finished. Very little changed until the late 1840s with the influx of German craftsmen and Irish laborers. Many of the newcomers found jobs at the Navy Yard. Even more worked on the expansion of the Capitol building, which began in 1851 and continued for fifteen years.

Waves of post-Civil War speculation and new construction gradually turned the Hill into what exists today. Many speculative developers built thousands of brick row houses to accommodate the city's burgeoning civil service workforce. Like today, the Hill's proximity to downtown and easy access to public transportation—horse-drawn and, later, motorized streetcars—increased the mobility of residents and made the Hill an attractive place to live.

The unifying factor in the social history of the Hill is that it has never lost its diversity. It has experienced in full measure the various waves of immigration to America's shores since 1791. One of the last came at the end of the nineteenth century when Eastern European Jews seeking freedom from persecution found their way to the Eighth Street, SE, commercial corridor now known as Barracks Row. In the early 1950s, many African Americans who had been displaced by massive urban renewal in southwest Washington also relocated to Capitol Hill. Today, the Hill retains its middle-class character.

Nowhere else in Washington is L'Enfant's original street plan better preserved than on Capitol Hill. The structures within the historic district reflect more than a century of architectural styles: Federal, Italianate, Second Empire, Romanesque, Queen Anne, and Classical Revival. Compared to in-town neighborhoods in other East Coast cities, Capitol Hill has a unique appearance: wide streets, bay fronts, iron-fenced front yards, ubiquitous red brick fired from iron-rich clay, elaborate ornamental pressed-brick facades adjacent to simple, unadorned frame buildings. Overall, a feeling of spaciousness is one of the key attractions of Capitol Hill. Many row houses are built in small groups while others occupy long, uninterrupted blocks. Imaginative and varied facades reveal the aspirations of the nineteenth-century middle-class residents. The Capitol Hill community enjoyed an amount of stability and security that was unusual in the late 1800s, and its architecture faithfully reflects the conservative values and qualities of its inhabitants.

Most Capitol Hill houses are row houses, with common walls and either front or rear gardens. Builders, often neighborhood residents, constructed most of the houses using architectural pattern books that illustrated various styles and instructed how to achieve the desired effect. By the time most of the existing houses were built after 1850, two innovations—cheap, machine-made nails

and mass production of standard sizes of lumber—had radically altered the building process. No longer did the construction of a house depend on the skills and knowledge of a master housewright. Building supply catalogs listed everything from iron roof systems and cast iron fronts to decorative window glass. The growth of nineteenth-century technology made variety and machine reproduction possible and brought architectural refinement within the financial means of a large segment of the population.

One of the earliest laws that affected the nature of Capitol Hill houses was George Washington's Wall Proclamation of 1791. This act allowed each builder to put one half of his wall on the adjoining property line and encouraged the building of row houses. The early District of Columbia commissioners had some exacting standards for building row houses. They wished, for example, to minimize fire hazards and so encouraged building brick houses. They soon realized, however, that "mechanics" and other workers could not afford the brick houses, so the commissioners decided to allow frame houses to be built as well.

The iron-fenced front yards of Capitol Hill are the result of another law. When L'Enfant laid out the city of Washington, he planned that the average street would be at least one hundred feet wide. But after the Civil War, the tremendous cost of paving such

wide streets led the city government to enact the "Parking Act" in 1870. An owner was allowed to fence or enclose all of the unused space in front of his house. And so, the front gardens of Capitol Hill houses are usually on public property.

A year later, the City Council decided to allow owners to build certain projections such as bays and towers four feet beyond the property line. Porches and steps could extend even farther onto public property. Towers, bays, and porches soon became common features of Capitol Hill houses—both the new and "modernized" older ones.

Battles have been fought and won by the community over highways that would have split the Hill, high rises that would have destroyed its streetscape, local government efforts to demolish the Eastern Market, and the federal government's plans to turn East Capitol Street—the center of the Hill—into a boulevard of government offices. A multitude of other threats could have destroyed the Hill if the community had not been vigilant and united.

Today, a person can tour Capitol Hill, admire the lovely old homes and colorful little fenced yards, delight in the pleasures of urban living, and enjoy the rich heritage of this beloved neighborhood in the shadow of the great Capitol.

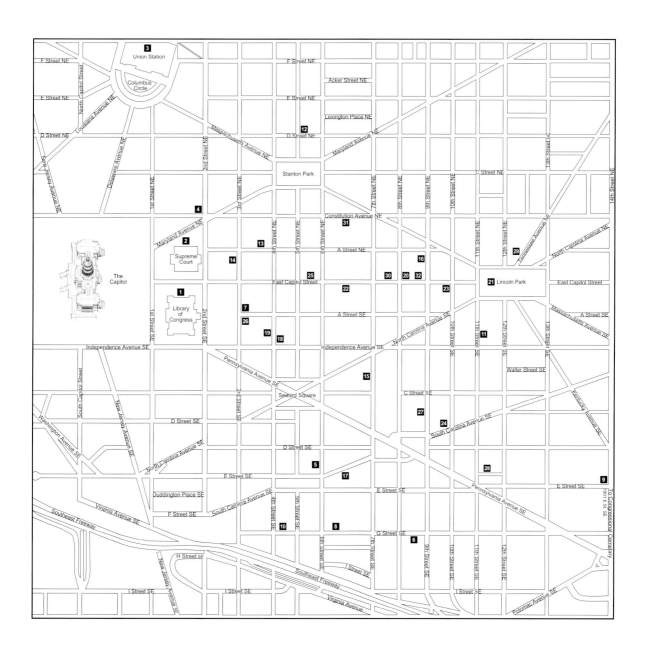

Gateway to Historic Capitol Hill

The gateway to the historic Capitol Hill neighborhood is distinguished by three of the most magnificent buildings in America: the Library of Congress, the Supreme Court, and Union Station.

Library of Congress—Thomas Jefferson Building
First Street and Independence Avenue, SE

The stunning Thomas Jefferson Building, the first of the three Library of Congress structures on Capitol Hill, was completed in 1897. It is a brilliant fusion of literature and art, and a dramatic reminder of the nation's debt to past Western civilizations.

The exuberant Beaux-Arts architecture on the exterior is a prelude to a riot of mural decoration and sculptural figures on the interior extolling the progress of human knowledge. A mountain of gray New Hampshire granite was transformed by more than forty artists and craftsmen into a sacred depository of knowledge and creativity for future generations, and a symbol of late nineteenth-century American optimism. The Italian Renaissance-style building based on the Paris Opera House was designed by Washington architects John L. Smithmeyer and Paul J. Pelz.

With more than 126 million items, the Library of Congress ranks as the largest library in the world and the nation's oldest federal cultural institution.

Supreme Court
First and East Capitol Streets, NE

Since its completion in 1935, the U.S. Supreme Court building—with its imposing entrance stairs, soaring columns, and sculptural pediment—has epitomized the American courthouse. Following a dictum laid down by Thomas Jefferson that federal architecture should be in the classical style of Greece and Rome, architect Cass Gilbert looked back to ancient Rome to create an iconic building reflecting democratic ideals.

The building is composed of three parts: a dominant temple of Roman derivation flanked by two wide horizontal wings. The entire composition is a carefully constructed procession beginning at the sidewalk where a visitor climbs a few low-rise stairs to a one hundred-foot-wide oval plaza, ascends a full-story staircase onto a portico with sixteen massive columns—an American variant of the Corinthian order—passing through imposing bronze doors into a colonnaded main hall that culminates at the far end in the dignified court chamber.

Throughout the route to the entrance, a visitor is surrounded by white Vermont marble with unusually high mica content, causing blinding reflections on sunny days. White glazed roof tiles add to the luminous appearance of the building.

Union Station
Columbus Circle at First Street and Massachusetts Avenue, NE

"Make no little plans; they have no magic to stir men's blood . . ." said Daniel Burnham, the architect of Union Station and one of America's most eminent Beaux-Arts architects.

To fulfill and expand Peter L'Enfant's grand vision for the national Mall, Burnham was instrumental in persuading railroads to abandon their unsightly stations at the foot of Capitol Hill and build one station—Union Station—just north of the Capitol.

Begun in 1903, the grand Beaux-Arts building opened in 1907 as the largest railroad station in the world. Burnham combined two ancient architectural typologies to create the building: the triumphal arch and the public bath. The design is based on Rome's Arch of Constantine and the Baths of Diocletian, with allegorical figures sculpted by Louis Saint-Gaudens that represent Fire, Electricity, Freedom, Imagination, Agriculture, and Mechanics. With the decline of railroad passenger service, the building was nearly lost, but in 1988 the station was restored to its former glory and reopened as a transportation hub and bustling retail center that serves not only as a destination for the millions of visitors who come to Washington each year but also as an exciting neighborhood watering hole for Hill residents.

Sewall-Belmont House

144 Constitution Avenue, NE

One of the oldest houses on Capitol Hill, this Federal-style mansion was built by Maryland plantation owner Robert Sewall in 1800. Sewall rented the house to Albert Gallatin, secretary of the treasury under Jefferson and Madison, who lived there with his family from 1801 to 1813. On August 24, 1814, American flotillamen occupying the house fired on British troops invading Washington, and so the British set fire to the house, destroying the front two rooms before a thunderstorm doused the flames. Sewall rebuilt the house, and it remained in the family until 1922 when Senator Porter Dale of Vermont purchased and restored it.

In 1929, Dale sold the property to the National Woman's Party, and it has remained the organization's headquarters ever since. The party renamed the structure the Sewall-Belmont House to honor Alva Belmont, whose financial contribution enabled its purchase. The house also served as the residence of the party's legendary founder, Alice Paul, until her death in 1972.

The balanced three-bay facade retains its Federal-style detail and original Flemish bond walls. The mansard roof with three dormer windows was added in the late nineteenth century, and the exterior staircase dates from the early twentieth century.

A peacock stained-glass fanlight was added to the entrance in the late nineteenth century.

Busts and portraits of the leaders of the American Woman's Suffrage Movement are the centerpieces of the entrance hall.

This was the desk of Susan B. Anthony, who drafted the nineteenth amendment to the Constitution.

A bust of suffragist Susan B. Anthony, done by longtime Hill resident and sculptor Adelaide Johnson, who also created the Portrait Monument statue of suffrage pioneers in the Capitol rotunda.

The main drawing room is the California Room in honor of Phoebe Hearst, whose son William Randolph Hearst donated the Victorian-era furniture. On the pedestal is a bust of suffragist Lucretia Mott by Adelaide Johnson.

Sparatt House
421½ Sixth Street, SE

Through the windows of this classic Federal-style house, two centuries of inhabitants have witnessed the transformation of pastoral Jenkins Hill into urban Capitol Hill. The house was completed in 1802 by Hugh Densley, a master plasterer who was one of the city's earliest craftsmen. In addition to working as a plasterer on the White House and the Capitol, he engaged in residential real estate development. Densley sold this finished house to Joseph Sparatt, the owner of a grocery store.

Despite more than two hundred years of shifts in architectural fashion, the house has steadfastly remained true to its origins. The simple doorway with arched fanlight above, Flemish bond brick, stone lintels with keystones, and gable roof with a dormer make it a fine example of a Federal-style townhouse. The original cast-iron hitching post remains at the front curb.

Densley also built the adjoining Carbery House, which was owned by Washington Mayor Thomas Carbery. The Carbery House, however, was dramatically changed from its original Federal style into the popular picturesque Victorian villa style in 1881 with the addition of a central tower and porch.

An arched porch topped with a soaring tower virtually disguises the Federal-style origins of the Carbery House, also built by Hugh Densley, that adjoins the Sparatt House.

The interior remains largely intact except for this kitchen, which was moved from the basement to this former dining room. The dumbwaiter was in the far right corner.

A simple fanlight and wide-plank pine floors in the entrance hall help attest to the two hundred-year-old origins of the house.

Simple furnishings complement the chaste architecture and modest proportions of the rooms.

Marine Corps Commandant's House
801 G Street, SE

While on a horseback outing one spring day in 1801, Pres. Thomas Jefferson and the Marine Corps's second commandant, William Ward Barrows, selected this site as the permanent location for the Marine Corps garrison and the official residence of the commandant. The site was considered ideal as it was within easy marching distance of the Capitol and a short walk from the Navy Yard.

The Georgian Federal-style house was completed in 1806. It is attributed to George Hadfield, who designed the Custis-Lee Mansion in Arlington National Cemetery and was the second superintendent of construction on the Capitol. The residence is the oldest public building in continuous use in Washington and the only structure left of the original construction, as the barracks was replaced in the early 1900s.

The original house measured twenty-five-by-thirty-two feet with four large rooms and a central hallway on both of two floors with a third floor attic. Renovations and additions, which began in 1836, expanded the house to fifteen thousand square feet with thirty rooms. The most notable changes were made in 1901 when the mansard roof and dormers were added, giving the roofline a Second Empire form.

A marker in front of the house shows it was designated a National Historic Landmark in 1976.

The back of the house overlooks the barracks parade grounds. A solarium was added across the back in 1907.

Adjoining parlors occupy the rear portion of the first floor. Portraits of former commandants line the walls.

The second parlor is used as a music room. Both parlors open to a solarium across the back of the house.

The elegant dining room features a 1983 painting by Col. Charles Waterhouse showing the house before it was enlarged in 1837 and the brick was painted the current white color.

A niche in the dining room displays export china belonging to Archibald Henderson, the Grand Old Man of the Marine Corps, who served as commandant from 1820 to 1859.

A signed photograph of H.R.H. Prince Philip is on a table in the guest room.

A lady's sitting room is just off the entrance hall.

This guest room is named in honor of H.R.H. Prince Philip of Great Britain, who occupied it during his visit for the American bicentennial.

Handy-Clements House
300 A Street, SE

Nestled among towering Victorian structures, this genteel center-hall Greek Revival-style house occupies a double lot on a prominent corner just behind the Library of Congress. The house, flanked by gardens of boxwood and ivy, was started around 1800.

The simple frame structure originally consisted of just two floors, two rooms deep on the back. The front four rooms were added a few years later. Interestingly, the porch, with the fluted Doric columns that give the house its distinctive and charming style, was not added until the early twentieth century. Typical of many vernacular-style houses built along the eastern seaboard during this period, the structure retains the low seven-and-a-half-foot ceilings and six-and-a-half-foot doorways trimmed with bull's eye molding.

The house was the residence of physician William E. Handy and his wife Isabel in the middle to late 1800s. Robert E. Clements and his wife Hattie owned the house for the first half of the twentieth century, and it remained largely unchanged until 1965. The current owner—attracted to the cozy rooms with comfortable proportions and abundant light on three sides—purchased the house from the estate of Hattie Clements and undertook extensive renovations.

In a cozy den, Santos carvings from South America and Native American pottery on the mantel surround a Polish winter landscape.

A two-sided fireplace provides a warm glow to the dining room with its French provincial furniture.

Treasured heirlooms include a beautiful 1860s Alsatian walnut corner cabinet and German oil painting. A Belle Époque Louis XVI-style bergère provides comfortable seating.

The living room is filled with antique French furniture. Louis Comfort Tiffany-design mosaics share the walls with family paintings from Germany.

The quaint kitchen has an early nineteenth-century brick hearth with a terra cotta floor and beamed ceiling.

The focal point of the powder room is a large Victorian pedestal basin.

Christ Church
620 G Street, SE

Organized in 1794, Christ Church is the oldest church chartered in the Federal City of Washington. It came as close to being a state church as the nation would ever have. Presidents Jefferson, Madison, Monroe, and John Quincy Adams worshiped here. It was also the official church of the Marine Band and the Marines, who marched here every Sunday morning from their barracks less than two blocks away and sat in the balcony.

The original 1807 building was a simple two-story Flemish bond brick structure with pointed arch windows and a vaulted cove ceiling. Although often attributed to Benjamin Latrobe, it was actually designed by Robert Alexander, a member of the vestry and chief contractor for the nearby Navy Yard.

Successive architects expanded the building to create one of the first Gothic Revival structures in the United States. In 1824, the rear portion was extended, and in 1849 the narthex and bell tower were added. Another notable change came in 1868 when pebble dash stucco was applied to the structure. The bell tower, which was extended in 1891, is punctuated with a projecting pointed-arch entrance vestibule flanked with small lancet windows.

Congressional Cemetery
1801 E Street, SE

Congressional Cemetery is America's oldest national cemetery. Established in 1807 by Capitol Hill residents, it was turned over to Christ Church in 1812. Four years later, part of the cemetery was selected for internment of members of Congress, and the grounds have been known ever since as Congressional Cemetery.

For many years, it was referred to as the "American Westminster Abbey," as it was the nation's leading burial grounds before Arlington National Cemetery was established. The thirty-three-acre cemetery is the resting place of such prominent figures as Elbridge Gerry, signer of the Declaration of Independence and vice president of the United States; William Thornton, designer of the U.S. Capitol; Mathew Brady, celebrated Civil War photographer; and John Philip Sousa, U.S. Marine Band leader and noted composer.

A distinctive feature of the cemetery is the rows of identical cenotaphs commemorating members of Congress who died in office from 1807 to 1877. Famed architect Benjamin Latrobe designed the sandstone monuments with their massive square bases surmounted with conical caps. Another prominent feature is the Public Vault built in 1835. National figures such as John Quincy Adams, William Henry Harrison, Zachary Taylor, and Dolley Madison were temporarily interred in the vault until they could be moved to family plots in their home states.

The "March King" John Philip Sousa, leader of the U.S. Marine Band from 1880 to 1892, is buried in this grave. Sousa was born and raised on Capitol Hill.

An early-nineteenth-century family vault in Greek Revival style.

Metheney-Cardinale House
408 G Street, SE

This frame house with a charming front porch is half of a duplex built around the time of the Civil War. The pitched roof is one indication of its early construction date, as houses built later in the century typically had flat sheet metal roofs.

Originally the house consisted of just four rooms—a front and back room on two floors. In 1899, the front porch was added to bring the house in line with others on the block. The porch helped create a separation between the street and the house, providing a transition from the public to the private spheres. In the mid-twentieth century, the freestanding summer kitchen was joined to the back of the house. The bathroom was added behind the kitchen at a later date and retains the original pipes and fixtures.

As with many Capitol Hill houses, the same family owned the home for decades. Antonio and Maria Cardinale moved into this residence in 1920 and lived there into the 1970s. Today, the house retains many of its nineteenth-century features while showcasing the eclectic collections and treasures of its artist-owner.

Reminiscent of a typical Victorian interior, the rooms of the house are filled with furniture, bric-a-brac, and art from various cultures.

On the left, a painting by aboriginal artist Rover Thomas hangs above one of Santa Fe artist Naida Seibel's bird men sculptures. A pair of Persian landscapes painted by Harold Weston in 1919 hangs just above a carved Mexican bench.

Paintings in the studio reflect the owner's various interpretations of nature.

Talavera ceramics by the Uriarte family of Puebla, Mexico, fill the kitchen. This colorful majolica earthenware is made using the same techniques developed in sixteenth-century Spain.

Philadelphia Row
124-154 Eleventh Street, SE

This row of Federal-looking townhouses is home to Capitol Hill's most enduring love story. Legend has it that in 1866 Charles Gessford, a carpenter and one of the most prolific builders on Capitol Hill, constructed this row of sixteen townhouses in a Philadelphia style so his wife, raised in the City of Brotherly Love, could look out across the street from their home and be reminded of her native city. In fact, wealthy Philadelphia tugboat manufacturer and speculator Stephen Flanagan constructed the houses in 1862 on speculation.

The houses were unique for the Hill. They were lower to the ground than other rows of the same period and had marble foundations and steps. Their flat fronts were made from smooth, machine-made red bricks. Unlike classic Federal-style buildings that required strict symmetry, these houses possessed a subtle asymmetry and unusual rhythm. Flat roofs invisible from the streets, modest brackets at the cornice line, white stone sills and lintels, four-panel doors, and larger windowpanes further distinguished these houses from their Hill forebears. The row's location, a mile east of the Capitol just off Lincoln Park, anticipated by at least thirty years a new center of population for the Hill. It took until 1897 for Flanagan to sell the last of his houses.

A magnificent late nineteenth-century German tall clock next to a Kuwaiti chest fill a corner of the living room. An aged Heriz carpet provides a pattern of soft color throughout the room.

At #138, the living room retains its original marble mantel. Sheers at the windows allow light to flood the room, highlighting the early- to mid-nineteenth-century furniture.

At #154, the Victorian character of the room has been altered by replacing the original carved marble mantel with a simple wood Federal-style mantelpiece.

Window valences with floor-length drapes give a classic formality to the living room with its comfortable mid-twentieth-century upholstered furniture.

At #138, a long, side entrance hall leads to a cross-hall with an unusual corkscrew staircase, a unique feature of Philadelphia Row houses.

The dining room in these row houses is usually off the cross-hall in the center of the first floor. At #154, antique Hitchcock chairs are matched with a contemporary Parsons table.

Barrett House
401 Fifth Street, NE

Thomas and Catharine Barrett's rural Civil War-era house started as a small two-story frame structure with four equal-sized rooms connected by a center hall. Today, numerous additions have tripled the size of the house and turned it into a striking urban residence.

The first major change came in 1875 when Mrs. Barrett, by this time a widow, moved the house to the corner of the large lot. A two-story structure was added on one side to accommodate a kitchen and bathroom. The stucco and wood trim ornamentation were also applied to give the house a more sophisticated appearance.

Another dramatic alteration came in 1908 when Robert Clements raised the house and constructed a full-story brick ground floor with a storefront bay facing the side street to house a grocery store. By the end of the twentieth century, the house had deteriorated badly. The ground floor was a storefront church, and the upper floors were apartments.

Childhood memories of Charleston's side gardens and Savannah's double entrance staircases inspired the current owners to incorporate the architectural flavor of these two cities when they undertook major renovations in 1994. The owners gutted the structure, built another two-story addition, and created a new interior that takes advantage of the abundant light on three sides.

A Sheraton-style mirror hangs above a mantelpiece with a simple Greek-key motif. Inside the fireplace rests a pair of charming porcelain dolphin andirons.

The formal living room is anchored by an American Empire secretary and upholstered armchair.

Alice, the mistress of the house, surveys her domain while being watched over by a mid-nineteenth-century painting of a Madonna above a circa 1820s Pembroke table.

A gold Neoclassical-style mirror reflects the fireplace, which is flanked by a niche with Japanese Imari and blue and white porcelain from China, England, and France.

The dining room table gleams with green and gold Wedgwood china and a combination of American and European silver and crystal.

Nostalgic Roof, a gift from Austrian artist Hundertwasser, has a special corner in the dining room.

Centennial Queen Anne side chairs surround a Hepplewhite-style dining table. The Sheraton secretary dates from the late eighteenth century.

A bronze replica of a stone lion sculpted by Isidore Bonheur is flanked by Napoleon III marble urns on the mantel in the master bedroom sitting room.

The master bedroom's cozy sitting room has a spiral staircase leading to a roof deck that provides a panoramic view of the city.

Frederick Douglass House
316-318 A Street, NE

In 1871, famed statesman and prominent abolitionist Frederick Douglass moved to Washington and purchased an Italianate-style residence at 316 A Street, NE, for his home. Two years later, he bought the adjacent house at 318. Douglass lived and worked in the home until 1877 when he moved to Cedar Hill, a mansion in the Anacostia section of the city. The Capitol Hill property stayed in the Douglass family until the 1920s.

The two houses remained in private hands until the mid-1960s when former Foreign Service officer Warren Robbins established the Museum of African Art in them. In 1979, Robbins deeded the museum properties, an art collection of five thousand works, and an extensive photo archive on African art and culture as a gift to the Smithsonian Institution. Ten years later, to help offset the costs of the new African Art Museum being built on the national Mall, the Smithsonian Institution sold the property to the National Association for Home Care. The association restored the homes and created the Frederick Douglass Museum and Hall of Fame for Caring Americans.

The exteriors of the houses are little changed from when the Douglass family lived here in the 1870s. The French mansard roof was the latest architectural fashion of the time.

The desk holds some of Douglass's papers, including his "freed man" paper signed by President Lincoln and an invitation to the dedication ceremonies for the Washington Monument in 1885. Above the desk is an original lithograph of President Lincoln delivering his first reading of the Emancipation Proclamation to members of his cabinet.

The parlor has several of Douglass's personal effects, including his writing desk, chair, and book press. The large photograph above the cabinet shows Douglass in front of his home. It is flanked by family portraits.

Lowell-Tisdel House
24 Third Street, NE

This two-story frame house is a good example of a working-class residence in Washington from the late nineteenth century. The structure has the standard features of a simple Italianate row house: low roof, flat front with overhanging eaves supported by decorative brackets, and a one-story porch with incised scroll sawn post brackets. Large two-over-two, floor-to-ceiling windows bring natural light into the row house. The Italianate style was extremely popular on Capitol Hill from 1850 to 1880, and many variations—from this simple structure to the highly ornate "bracketed" style—can be seen throughout the historic district.

When clerk-turned-carpenter Thurston Lowell built the house in 1872, it was one of seven in a row. Though not identical, the buildings were similar in design and came to be called "Washington Terrace," probably referring to the slight hill or terrace rise upon which the lots sit. The designation was abandoned by 1910 once the neighborhood had been developed.

In 1873, the house was occupied by Willard P. Tisdel, second assistant marshal at the U.S. Supreme Court. Sen. Joseph McCarthy lived in one of the houses during the 1954 Army-McCarthy hearings, and the U.S. attorney general resides on the row today.

The picturesque porch has scroll sawn post brackets in a flower motif and a refreshing blue ceiling.

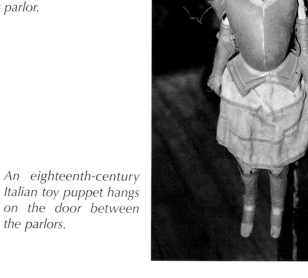

Vibrant coral walls with white plantation window shutters create a wonderful background for a mix of furnishings, including a freeze-dried palm tree, in the front parlor.

An eighteenth-century Italian toy puppet hangs on the door between the parlors.

Connecting parlors off the side entrance hall allow for grand entertaining. Random-width pine floors with aged oriental carpets give warmth to the rooms.

A quarter sawn oak corner cabinet from Virginia stands behind a settee affectionately called "the twins." Above the mantel hang chinoiserie panels.

A view from the front parlor into the adjoining back parlor reveals a continuation of the comfortable, eclectic style of the rooms.

A 1740 English tall clock reflects reverse-painted pictures over the dining room mantel.

The entrance hall leads to a large formal dining room with a corner fireplace.

The back staircase has a wonderful Chinese Chippendale-style stair railing. An Italian carving of Jesus is displayed on the pedestal.

The master bathroom features a claw and ball foot porcelain tub and random-width pine flooring.

Spare and simple, the master bedroom has a fresh and serene country air.

Eastern Market
Seventh and C Streets, SE

Washington once boasted several huge markets for fresh meat, fish, eggs, cream, bread, and fruit. Peter L'Enfant envisioned farmers' markets throughout the city as a focus of commercial activity. Today, the Eastern Market is one of the few remaining public markets in the nation's capital.

Constructed in 1873, the building was designed by Adolph Cluss, a prominent local architect who was also responsible for the Smithsonian Arts and Industries Building. The one-story structure is twenty bays long and five bays deep with a hip monitor roof covered by gray slate shingles. The outstanding architectural characteristic is the adaptation of its red brick cladding to a round-arch style. Narrow bays with doors surmounted by large bull's eye windows alternate with wider sunken window bays. The corbelled brick cornice is supplemented on the projecting entrance bay by massive, double wood brackets carrying a deep overhanging molded wood cornice.

The single volume interior is remarkably unchanged with its iron bar trusses supporting the exposed roof. An addition on the north dates from 1908.

Fresh flowers are weekend staples at the market under the open shed along Seventh Street.

On Saturday and Sunday, vendors set up stalls to sell everything from antique furniture and prints to clothing and hand-made jewelry.

Rothwell House
25 Ninth Street, NE

This picture-perfect Second Empire house was built in 1874 by Richard Rothwell as a family home for his wife and seven children. Rothwell was a stonemason who worked on the Civil War-era extension of the Capitol and later the post-war Pension Building, now the National Building Museum. This house is a product of America's post-Civil War flirtation with French architecture. Few examples of this style exist on Capitol Hill because its popularity predates the Hill's major development. The house's corner location allowed a full expression of the grandeur of the style. Classic elements include the slate mansard roof with dormers, dressed stone facade with corner quoins, filigreed balcony, and keystone arches.

Many Capitol Hill denizens know this residence as the "Buffalo Bill house." The legendary William F. Cody often stayed here, dividing his time between performing in his Wild West Show and attempting to convince Congress that Native Americans needed federal aid. Rothwell's son-in-law, Col. John H. Peake, an aide to Gen. George Custer in the Civil War, was a business partner of William Cody. Pres. James Garfield is reputed to have visited the house frequently. The last occupants of the house before the current owners began restoration in 1973 were part of the "plumbers" of the Nixon administration's Watergate scandal.

The kitchen's no-nonsense professional look includes white cabinets, granite counters and back splash, and small octagonal-shaped ceramic floor tiles. Copper pots gleam over an industrial stove.

A small foyer opens to a long narrow side hall that serves as a picture gallery leading to a kitchen with a surprising high curved ceiling of wood slates punctuated with a skylight.

The first floor has been restored to reflect its Victorian origin. The plaster crown molding was painstakingly duplicated.

Over the mantel and throughout the house is a collection of landscape paintings by Utah artist Leconte Stewart.

In the living room, oriental furnishings mingle with antiques and contemporary art. Over the sofa hangs an early oil painting by Lee Deffebach.

A detail of the magnificent Victorian-era bed.

A guest room is decorated with baroque furnishings in burled wood. The ornate bed and dresser are thought to have belonged to William Jennings Bryan.

The den has Wassily chairs by Marcel Breuer and a square glass Barcelona table designed by Mies van der Rohe.

The den was designed to accommodate the wall-size artwork of Slaithong Schmutzhart, a Washington artist who used to be the owner's neighbor.

Woods House
613 South Carolina Avenue, SE

Andrew Woods, a machinist at the Washington Navy Yard, built this house in 1849 and enlarged the eighteen-foot-wide structure and added the intricate ornamentation in 1877. That dramatic makeover transformed this plain early Victorian-era residence into a high-styled "bracketed Italianate" with prominent window eyebrows. The additions included a white painted lacy wooden door hold, cast-metal lintels over the windows, and a wooden overhanging cornice with molding supported by brackets and adorned with medallions. These were typical middle-class amenities of the period.

In 1958, the house was remodeled and most of the nineteenth-century interior details were stripped away.

In the mid-1980s, Capitol Hill architect Hector Alvarez nearly doubled the size of the house for the current owners with additions and modifications in a contemporary spirit but with physical characteristics of Victorian architecture. Alvarez added symmetrical wings that he set back from the façade to avoid competing with it. Each new wing has a separate entrance in a bay that recalls Victorian style. The result echoes the strong vertical lines of the 1877 facade and adds light as well.

The mahogany stair rail with turned balusters and octagonal newel post is the only remaining nineteenth-century interior detail. The fireplace was given a curved facing to break up the rectangular lines of the room.

A freestanding column in the far corner of the living room creates a small vestibule at the front door and serves as a coat closet on one side and a niche for art on the other.

The column form in the living room is repeated in a new stairwell connecting the kitchen and the upstairs back hall, and in the curve in the kitchen table

The dining room occupies the ground floor of one of the new additions. An ocular window looks out onto a backyard patio.

Larman-Costaggini House
120 Fourth Street, SE

This elegant, high-styled Italianate house with elaborate bracketed wood cornice, exuberant cast iron eyebrows painted to look like stone, and distinctive brownstone steps was built in 1874. Its owner was Henry Larman, the sanitary engineer for the city's legendary Alexander "Boss" Shepherd—the man who modernized Washington by laying miles of sewers and roads, as well as installing the first gas lines.

In the 1880s, artist Filippo Costaggini occupied the house. He was the pupil of Constantino Brumidi, the Italian artist responsible for murals in the Capitol and the frescoes in the Rotunda that depict great events in American history. Costaggini worked on the frescoes from 1880 to 1888, finishing the frieze begun by Brumidi.

The current owner of this house is a pioneer. Long before the Capitol Hill Historic District was created in 1976 and Victorian-era architecture came to be appreciated, he recognized the value of Capitol Hill and its architectural treasures. In 1957, when he purchased this "tired old lady," it had shutters and was painted white to look like a Colonial structure. He painstakingly restored the house and returned its aristocratic bearing.

Walnut entrance doors are highlighted by lanterns from an old funeral coach. Ornamental cast-iron window brackets were once part of architect Stanford White's New York City townhouse.

The grand piano was the Chickering Company's "presentation piece" at the Chicago Exposition of 1881. Above it hangs a nineteenth-century Louis Philippe clock, one of forty-three antique clocks found throughout the house.

The immense drawing room, affectionately called the "big saloon parlor," has an ornate plaster strapwork ceiling with a crystal gasolier that has been electrified.

One of a pair of original Carrara marble mantelpieces surmounted by matched, walnut-framed pier mirrors highlights the parlor.

A magnificent eighteenth-century Dutch marquetry chest occupies the wall between the fireplaces. Above it are early twentieth-century aquatints of Paris and Prague by Czechoslovakian artist T. Frantisek Simon.

A tubular tall case clock and banjo clock share walls lined with fine paintings and mirrors in the ground floor hall. A collection of walking canes is next to a mid-nineteenth-century curly maple ballroom chair.

Part of a collection of Russian, Italian, English, French, German, and Chinese boxes fashioned of gold, silver, brass, mother-of-pearl, mosaic, burled woods, and lacquer is displayed in the drawing room.

Lindbergh House
115 Fourth Street, SE

The street between this quaint Italianate house built in 1879 and the grand Larmer-Costaggini House across the street served as the playground for an American hero: Charles Augustus Lindbergh, Jr.

The boy was five years old when his father came to Washington in 1907 to represent the Sixth District of Minnesota. The senior Lindbergh remained in Congress for ten years. During that period, young Charles lived in Washington, eventually attending nearby Eastern High School. In 1927, more than nine thousand Washingtonians turned out to see their famous son when the USS *Memphis* carrying the "Lone Eagle" and his plane, the *Spirit of St. Louis*, home from their famous transatlantic flight, docked at the Navy Yard on Capitol Hill.

This house took advantage of the "Projection Act," passed by Congress in 1871, to maximize its size with a demi-octagonal bay window. The legislation allowed bay windows, corner towers, and porches to project into public space. Using projections, builders could construct larger houses on smaller lots and gain more light with extra windows in the bays. This also allowed greater freedom to incorporate many romantic and picturesque variations into the facades. Suddenly, staid Italianate-style houses had exuberant bays.

An eighteenth-century French painted and parcel-gilt trumeau mirror hangs above a Louis XV-style sofa.

The grand drawing room with its eleven-foot ceilings has some of the most elaborate original cast plaster cornices, strap work, and finials of any house on Capitol Hill.

A magnificent American gilt overmantel mirror, circa 1840, casts a reflection of the cornice detail through the room.

A mix of furnishings creates a very personal dining room: American Federal armoire, Louis XV-style armchairs, ladder-back side chairs, and a Waterford crystal chandelier. On the far wall, the painting of the figures is Mother Earth by Native American artist Richard Red Owl.

A luxurious master bath opens into the sitting room.

An eighteenth-century-style French tapestry hangs above a Chippendale sofa in the sitting room.

A Victorian rose-colored sitting room with a Louis XV-style fauteuil offers a comfortable place to relax. The mahogany linen press conceals a television.

A corner in the main hallway displays photographs and memorabilia related to the flying ace.

An up-to-date kitchen has a charming old-fashioned feeling with an oak Irish pub table in the center.

Whelpley House
800 East Capitol Street, NE

Freestanding houses are a rarity on the Hill. This grand three-story Italianate-style house on four lots was built in 1876 by James W. Whelpley, a clerk at the Treasury Department, for his wife Louisa and their children. In 1886, Pres. Grover Cleveland tapped Whelpley to be assistant treasurer of the United States. Whelpley later became president of the D.C. Board of Education and retired in 1915 as president of the Eastern Building and Loan Association. Upon his death in 1919, the house was sold, beginning a long and steady deterioration and loss of its architectural details.

From 1925 to 1931, the house served as the School for Feeble Minded Children, later changed to Atypical Public School. In 1947, a rooming house license was issued to allow multi-tenant housing in the structure, and, in 1961, it became an apartment building.

Fortunes reversed in 2000 when the house was sold to the present owners. They spent four years lovingly reconstructing it with great attention to recreating the original details. Today the house has come full circle, serving once again as a private residence for a growing family.

In 1905, Whelpley had this house built at the rear of the property for his son. Today, it is occupied by his great-granddaughter.

A photograph of the Whelpley family house in 1893 guided the current owners in their painstaking restoration of the house.

A small entry foyer opens into a center hall. The dining room and kitchen are on one side of the hall and there are double parlors on the other side.

A lithograph of larger-than-life magnolia blossoms by San Francisco artist Gary Bukovnik hangs over the dining room buffet.

Circa 1840s carved Empire host and hostess chairs frame the opening into the back parlor, now used as a family room. A solarium extends across the back of the house.

Intricately carved columns that match the posts on the front porch decorate the opening from the hall into the front parlor.

Lincoln Park
East Capitol Street between Eleventh and Thirteenth Streets

Lincoln Park marks the eastern end of the Capitol Hill Historic District. The square was set aside in Peter L'Enfant's plan of the city and was to be the location of a column from which all distances of places on the continent would be measured.

By the Civil War, however, the site was still undeveloped. Union soldiers camped here and a temporary hospital was set up. The square was nameless until 1867 when Congress authorized it to be called Lincoln Square in honor of the martyred president.

In 1876, President Grant and Frederick Douglass, then America's highest-ranking African American government official, dedicated the Emancipation Monument in the center of the park. The monument, by sculptor Thomas Ball, depicts a life-size Abraham Lincoln bidding a slave to rise to freedom. Lincoln stands with a copy of the Emancipation Proclamation in his right hand. The head of the slave was modeled from a photograph of Archer Alexander, the last African American captured under the Fugitive Slave Act.

From 1876 until 1922, when the Lincoln Memorial was dedicated, this park was the country's major memorial to Abraham Lincoln and a major tourist attraction.

In 1974, a statue honoring African American educator Mary McLeod Bethune was erected at the eastern end of the park.

The houses around the park span the period from 1885 to 1915.

McGill House
639 East Capitol Street, SE

East Capitol Street is Capitol Hill's grand avenue. An astonishing 160 feet wide, it was originally envisioned to be a ceremonial boulevard comparable to those in Paris, lined with grand embassies leading to the Capitol. In Peter L'Enfant's plan for the city, the mile between the Capitol and Lincoln Park was to be an avenue of shops, with each side of the street having an arcade for the comfort of customers. This concept never materialized, however, as the city grew to the west instead of the east.

It was not until after the Civil War that most of East Capitol Street developed, becoming a prime residential street rather than a commercial entranceway. Today the avenue has a ceremonial feeling, as the broad street with its spacious front gardens is lined with many of the largest and most stately houses in the historic district. The architecture of East Capitol Street tends to be more elaborate and exuberant than elsewhere on the Hill.

This statuesque three-story house was one of four built in 1878 by architect James H. McGill. It is a subtle transition from the ornate Italianate style to the more chaste Queen Anne style popular on the Hill after the 1880s. It features an elaborate metal corbel cornice and incised metal door brackets typical of the Italianate style but has refined brickwork characteristic of the Queen Anne period.

The house was featured in the 1987 film *Broadcast News.*

An American Empire bird's-eye maple chest converted into a washstand with an early Victorian gilt mirror makes an elegant powder room off the center hall.

In the living room, a New York Regency fancy chair and 1928 Art Deco ebony Bechstein grand piano are balanced by a Seth Thomas tall clock, circa 1814.

An ornately carved 1905 Classical Revival mantelpiece and fireplace tiles were salvaged from St. Matthew's Rectory in Washington. An eighteenth-century gilt Rococo-style prism mirror from France hangs above the fireplace.

The living room was relocated to the back of the house to take advantage of light on three sides and the garden view. Family antiques and pieces acquired while living in France have been placed over a nineteenth-century Kashgai carpet.

The phoenix, representing the wife, is shown with two chicks, representing the owners' daughters, in the dining room mural.

A detail of the dragon, representing the husband, in the dining room mural.

Over a Napoleon III oak cabinet is artist Michael Welzenbach's allegorical depiction of the family with a dragon representing the husband and a phoenix the wife.

The living room opens to a lush garden with a brick terrace and walkway leading to a two-story carriage house.

The original front parlor is now a dining room. An early twentieth-century maple table is set with eighteenth-century Canton china and surrounded by Duncan Phyfe chairs.

Fraunz House
923 East Capitol Street, SE

This soaring four-story residence built in 1882 is a classic Queen Anne-style row house. This style did not appear on Capitol Hill until 1880—more than a decade after its introduction elsewhere in the country—and was popular until the late 1890s.

Unlike the exuberant "painted ladies" of San Francisco, the Queen Anne houses on Capitol Hill were strait-laced, reflecting the conservative tastes of the Hill's predominant middle class. The houses were vertical in appearance and composed of dark red brick with long, narrow windows and distinguished by prominent bays, towers, or turrets topped by elaborate caps or, in the case of this house, a pediment.

While in other areas of the country the Queen Anne style was executed in a variety of wood siding and shingles, in Washington it was translated to variously patterned and textured machine-made pressed brick. These dense, extremely uniform bricks could be pressed into highly decorative molds for a variety of patterns and textures. These bricks also were less expensive than cut and carved stone, allowing builders to achieve great decorative effect at modest expense. A look around Capitol Hill reveals an extraordinary variety of pressed brick patterns. This house is a good example of the numerous patterns and textures achieved in brick in a Queen Anne house.

Machine-made pressed brick fashioned into various patterns was the major decorative element in Capitol Hill Queen Anne houses. It expressed a non-elitist style of simple and honest construction that suited the Hill's middle-class sensibilities.

Double parlors with eleven-foot ceilings provide generous, yet intimate, rooms. A Willard-style banjo eglomise clock hangs above a Pembroke table, circa 1790.

In the front parlor, an 1820 double-glass mirror hangs above a Chippendale-style settee surrounded by a 1930 Nathan Margolis Queen Anne tea table and George III corner chair by contemporary cabinetmaker Stephen H. Smith.

The center parlor is anchored by a Sheraton-style sofa with Philadelphia Centennial Chippendale side chairs. The Hepplewhite secretary in the corner is circa 1800.

A late eighteenth-century tall case clock by George Hardy, made in Fraserburgh, Scotland, occupies a corner niche.

A palette of peach and white with an aged pine floor set off a cannonball bed and Connecticut tilt-top breakfast table, circa 1770, in the guest room.

The dining room reveals an enfilade to the front parlor. A 1930s Nichols Chinese Deco rug covers the pine floors. The oil painting depicts the bark Jennie Cushman *leaving Boston in 1873 bound for Lisbon.*

A two-pedestal mahogany dining table is surrounded by a set of Philadelphia Centennial Chippendale chairs. A Regency bull's eye mirror with a spread eagle crest is aligned with the mirror in the front parlor.

In the master bedroom, a George III block-front chest and a pair of George III ladder-back chairs are complemented by a Hepplewhite tall-post bed by Connecticut cabinetmaker Stephen H. Smith.

The sage palette of the master bedroom is carried into the sitting room. An early-nineteenth-century Eli Terry shelf clock by Mark Leavenworth & Co. rests on the mantel. In the corner stands a mahogany Centennial Hepplewhite tambour secretary.

Teague House
920 South Carolina Avenue, SE

A distinguished facade was given to this row house of the late nineteenth century by extending the widows to the floor and adding a handsome iron balcony. Its spacious forty-foot front yard is an example of a unique arrangement of government land ownership and citizen stewardship. Washington's generous street widths were an integral part of L'Enfant's conception of the city. Diagonal avenues radiating from major points like the Capitol and White House were superimposed on an orthogonal grid of numbered and lettered streets. The diagonal avenues were named for states and were 120 to 160 feet wide compared to ninety to 112 feet for streets.

Prior to the Civil War, the city—and particularly Capitol Hill—grew slowly, and most streets were unpaved. By the late 1860s, Congress recognized that grading and paving the wide streets was unlikely to happen because of the exorbitant cost. So, in 1870, it passed the "Parking Act," allowing owners to use the land between the sidewalk line and the front property line, which for most Capitol Hill buildings is at the front door, and in 1899 permitted this area to be enclosed with short open fences. Today, these colorful front yards give Capitol Hill an open, gracious feeling that ties the divergent architectural styles of the buildings into a whole.

A mid-nineteenth-century Greco-Roman woodcarving resides in a dining room niche above a Chippendale-style side chair with a Marlborough foot. The dramatic landscape painting is by Cape Cod artist Robert Cardinal.

Two rooms were joined to create an expansive living room/dining room. An early-nineteenth-century flame mahogany American Empire buffet provides a transition between the two areas.

French moderne-style club chairs set a masculine tone in the living room. Maryland artist Cathy Yrizarry's painting of the rooftops of Canton, a Baltimore neighborhood, hangs over the fireplace. The small landscapes are by Robert Cardinal.

Painted wainscoting gives the living room a contemporary feeling. A nineteenth-century American Empire pillar and scroll game table is the perfect height for a sofa table.

A Corinthian capital makes a perfect—and apropos—beside table for a Capitol Hill home.

Unadorned windows with painted shutters and a pine wainscoting headboard create a clean, crisp look in the master bedroom. Over the bed is an engraving of York Cathedral. A delightful 1930s toy car is parked between the windows.

Doolittle-Tullock House
506 East Capitol Street, NE

George Doolittle would not recognize the transformation of his plain 1873 home into one of the most fashionable Victorian residences on Capitol Hill. In 1887, S. W. Tullock made radical changes, adding large front rooms on the first, second, and third floors, along with a loft on the fourth. Incorporating varied window patterns, highly textured materials, sweeping arches, and a dramatic roofline, Tullock turned the house into a fine example of Romanesque Revival. This style was popularized by prominent Boston architect Henry Hobson Richardson in the late 1800s. Exterior woodwork became less frequent and the strong vertical emphasis and other elements of the Queen Anne style were joined and sometimes replaced by a broad and massive style of architecture through the use of stone, arches, turrets, and medieval decorative elements.

The facade of the first floor of this house has a prominent arched-top transom and window of stained and leaded glass containing both American Aesthetic and Neoclassical elements framed by rusticated sandstone. The second story facade is dominated by an impressive pressed tin bay with Shingle-style small-paned, mullioned windows; the third story is recessed behind a sweeping arch to create a balcony; and the fourth story is capped by a steeply gabled roof that encloses a loft. The loft was used as a studio by Daniel Chester French, the sculptor who created the statue that dominates the interior of the Lincoln Memorial.

A pressed tin oriel (a bay window supported by a corbel) is one of the most striking features of the house.

The 1876 Centennial Exposition ushered in a revival of Federalist period furniture. This trend is reflected in Hepplewhite- and Sheraton-style furniture and gilt and eglomise looking glass with carved eagle, circa 1815.

The foyer and stair hall have rare chestnut wainscoting. Bird engravings are by English naturalist Mark Catesby from The Natural History of Carolina, Florida and the Bahama Islands, London, 1731-1743. A shield back side chair, circa 1800, is paired with a 1770 Chippendale crotch mahogany Pembroke table.

The arched stained glass window with a central crown of laurel leaves is an excellent example of the Romanesque Revival period.

Mid-nineteenth-century landscape paintings fill the walls of the front parlor. The oil painting on the left is an American landscape by William C. Frerichs. The one on the right is Cattle Watering in a Stream *by Charles François Daubigny, a leader of the naturalist Barbizon School. An antique Makal carpet complements the paintings.*

Botanical engravings in the dining room are by Basilius Besler from Hortus Eystettensis, *published in 1613.*

Chestnut wainscoting and a walnut coffered ceiling highlight the dining room. An early-eighteenth-century Hepplewhite sideboard and slant-top desk are joined by Centennial shield back chairs and a new Hepplewhite-style table.

A large bay window in the second floor library offers a sweeping vista down the street to the Capitol.

Brick-red walls in the library are a dramatic background for mid-nineteenth-century engravings of public buildings and monuments in Washington and Baltimore. The colors of the room are echoed in the circa 1890 Khamseh carpet.

Saint Mark's Church
Third and A Streets, SE

Designed by Baltimore architect T. Buckler Ghequier, this English Gothic Revival church was built in stages from 1888 to 1894. A dramatic 103-foot tower has buttresses on its two lower stages. An arched and balustraded open belfry, which is topped with corbelled corner turrets and gables, supports a hexagonal spire. The dark handmade brick is given a monochromatic textural richness through the use of molded terra-cotta belt courses in different widths and red Seneca sandstone trim. In 1930, a small chapel was added at the rear corner along the sidewalk.

A great baptistery window measuring 165-by-twenty-five feet by Louis C. Tiffany dominates the facade. It is one of the largest and oldest Tiffany windows ever made and a reproduction of the central section of *Christ Leaving the Praetorium* by nineteenth-century French illustrator Gustave Doré.

From 1896 to 1902, St. Mark's Church served as the Episcopal cathedral for the Diocese of Washington.

Claveloux House
313 Ninth Street, SE

The circa 1890 Queen Anne-style brick house with a square bay was very popular on Capitol Hill near the end of the Victorian era and can be seen with slight variations—primarily in size—throughout the neighborhood. Instead of the standard porches with fanciful woodwork and gingerbread trim in a riot of color that marked many Queen Anne houses, the Capitol Hill versions have a distinctive style. Steep cast-iron stairs lead to the main entrance a half story above the sidewalk. The open stairs allow light to filter down to an entrance under the stairs. Previously, the entrance went to a basement-level kitchen. Today the entrance is usually to a rental apartment. Other unusual features include simple railings and cutout patterned risers that are typically in a star, grape, or floral motif.

Hidden on the side and back of this particular house is a world quite uncommon on the Hill. Sun-filled rooms open onto a lush garden encircling a swimming pool. In 1990, local architect Amy Weinstein designed a one-story library/family room set back across the front of the house—now hidden by a giant southern magnolia tree—as well as a second-story addition on the back. The additions clearly distinguish themselves from the nineteenth-century materials and technology, yet speak the design language of the original building.

Yellow Abstract *by Capitol Hill artist Tati Kaupp gives a colorful focus to the garden room just off the living room.*

In the living room, a pair of Victorian-era marble fireplaces provides the focus for two seating areas. A Venetian glass chandelier lights a collection of Japanese woodblock prints on the back wall.

A brick floor and iron chandelier are bold contrasts to the elaborately carved fireplace and overmantel mirror. The striped column is by Santa Fe artist Naida Seibel.

The dining room has a contemporary formality with a glass table and oak Chippendale-style chairs. A Venetian chandelier over the table is reflected in an eighteenth-century Venetian mirror.

The den abounds with paintings by Capitol Hill artists. Tulips With Red Table Against Blue *by the owner hangs on the wall.*

The master bedroom features a simple armoire from Scotland joined by an elaborately carved chest and headboard from Mexico, where the owner lived before moving to the Hill.

*The master bathroom has a luxurious whirlpool tub overlooking the garden.
Glass frames filled with colorful butterflies bring nature inside.*

*Comfortable seating and shelves of books create a perfect sanctuary for reading
and catching the afternoon sun in the bedroom sitting area.*

Carpenter Gothic brackets, trusses, and pillars united by a gingko leaf motif evoke popular pattern book styles in vogue in the late nineteenth century.

A swimming pool surrounded by lush potted plants provides relief from the Washington summer heat and is a focal point for outdoor entertaining.

The Carriage House
414 Eleventh Street, SE

Life behind the main house has become a recent focus of many social researchers and a topic of much public fascination. Some 139 alleys on Capitol Hill offer a remarkable historic resource for exploring nineteenth-century life. Many alley dwellings and structures, dating primarily from 1877 to 1892, remain on the Hill and have been creatively adapted for today's lifestyles—giving the Hill a rich and vibrant "outback," as it were. A walk around the Hill reveals this intricate and inviting network: Brown's Court, Archibald Walk, Library Court, F Street Terrace, and Gessford Court, to name a few.

This 1890s carriage house, which is fortunate to include a street front entrance and secluded garden, has been modified to provide a large first-floor studio for its artist-owner with an open, loft-style residence above. Windows on all four sides provide abundant natural light and a sense of spaciousness.

A random arrangement of paintings in the studio makes a colorful photographic montage.

The ground floor—with its open space, high ceilings, and abundant light—makes a perfect artist's studio.

Aged pine floors and a white-painted beam ceiling with skylights create a casual feeling for the second-floor living space.

Overstuffed chairs and sofas anchor the large space on the second floor while providing ample seating.

An open kitchen at one end of the large room fosters an informal living and entertainment style.

Tucked to one side is the sleeping area. A whimsical chest of plywood and mahogany by the artist-owner rests at the foot of an iron bed that Huckle the cat finds most comfortable.

Strong-Egloff House
118 Tennessee Avenue, NE

"More! More!" was the mantra of the Victorian era. In architecture and the decorative arts, the Victorians kept adding and adding until virtually every surface was covered. From 1840 to 1900, American architecture saw the steady addition and assimilation of previous architectural styles from Romanesque to Gothic to Queen Anne into more and more exuberant and robust compositions.

This residence combines elements of late Victorian, particularly the pervasive Richardsonian Romanesque, and portends a more restrained future with its Neoclassical design. The generous thirty-six-foot-wide by thirty-eight-foot-deep house is built of dark red brick—now painted a cream color—and Indiana limestone. With its classical dentil cornice and sweeping roof balustrade, the handsome home remains as impressive today as when it was designed in 1898 by Capitol Hill architect Edwin P. Fowler and built for local businessman George W. Strong.

The Strongs lived in the house until 1906 when Julius Egloff, who had a saloon on Capitol Hill, became the second owner. The Egloff family remained in the house until 1936. This elegant house has served as a wonderful and spacious family home for the current owners for more than a quarter century.

A powder room occupies part of the former butler's pantry. A nineteenth-century German cabinet was converted into a washstand.

The entrance hall has a warm, cheery glow with feather-patterned walls that complement a tiger oak fireplace at the end. The console and mirror are late-nineteenth-century German.

A 1922 Baldwin grand piano is a favorite display space for framed photographs of family and friends. The bay still has the original curved wood curtain rod.

A magnificently carved oak fireplace mantel with a classical motif gives the library old world warmth and charm.

123

An eighteenth-century pearwood Chippendale chest and Chippendale-style armchair with scroll ears and a Rococo pierced splat contrast nicely with a Greek waterscape painting.

The formal parlor is centered on an elaborately carved classical fireplace that has been painted white to bring out its intricate details.

The parlor is filled with a wonderful arrangement of American and English furniture with colors that complement the oil painting on the right, which depicts the city of Toledo by Catalonian artist Josep Rovira-Brull.

The butler's pantry has been converted into a bar.

Formal meals are served on a banded mahogany Sheraton-style double pedestal table surrounded by Chippendale chairs. A window in the bay has been fitted with glass doors for direct access to the garden.

Highlighted by family photographs and an early-twentieth-century family quilt from Kentucky, a corner of the large second floor hall is a quiet place for reading.

The daughter's bedroom has a floral Arts and Crafts-style fireplace with an abundance of shelves and mirrors.

Statues of four muses grace the lush garden. Here, the muse of painting enjoys a sylvan setting by a flagstone pond.

A wine tasting room boasts an elaborately carved door from Washington's former haute French restaurant Leon d'Or that leads to the wine cellar.

Malnati House
712 East Capitol Street, NE

To long-time residents of Capitol Hill, this home is known as the "deer house" because of the life-size replica of a stag that has graced its spacious front garden for decades. Architect George S. Cooper designed the house in 1902 for Antonio Malnati, a builder and owner of a stone works, who constructed it for ten thousand dollars. Antonio Malnati died in 1906, but the family remained in the house until 1951. The house is unique for Capitol Hill in terms of its site, orientation, and architecture. The flat-front, three-story structure is built along the edge of a triple lot and is oriented to the long, open side with three large octagonal-shaped bays and a porch overlooking a side garden.

The Beaux-Arts architecture in a Second Renaissance Revival style is chaste, yet forceful. Constructed of a dark monochromatic brick over a brownstone base, the house is topped by a steep and dramatic terra cotta tiled roof accented by deeply stepped end gables. An imposing recessed stone entrance with a carved pediment dominates the facade. Large double-hung windows are punched directly into the brick. Over-scaled keystone brackets above the first-story windows and smaller ones connecting the second-floor windows to a simple stone entablature give a dramatic, idiosyncratic element to the exterior.

A delicate leaded-glass door brings an inviting glow into the entrance hall, whose scarlet wall covering and leopard print carpeting give a vibrant punch to the interior.

A gilded Italian mirror hangs above an early-twentieth-century inlaid French mahogany serpentine credenza with ormolu mounts in the entrance hall.

The kitchen continues the theme of mixing bold colors with warm wood tones. The leaded-glass cabinet doors match the design of the dining room display cabinets.

The bold colors and patterns in the living room are a striking contrast to the restrained exterior of the house. An ornate burl veneer display cabinet from the late 1800s contains a collection of elephants and donkeys.

A Staffordshire spill vase cow from the late 1800s has the words "MILK SOLD HERE," suggesting it might have been made for display in a store window.

Continental and American antique furnishings mixed with plump upholstered seating give a formal, but relaxed, atmosphere to the living room. Over the mantel hangs a copy of Jean-Francois Millet's Shepherdess with Her Flock by Ohio artist Robert J. Smith.

A collection of Boehm bird plates is the focal point in the leaded glass display cabinets. Cognac Jacquet, a vintage 1920 poster by Camille Bouchet, hangs in the hall.

American chestnut wainscoting, beam ceiling, and scarlet-colored walls create an inviting backdrop for a contemporary dining table and chairs in the Biedermeier style. A custom-made rug reflects the owner's love for color and flowers.

Parrot tulips, a favorite flower of the owner, are captured in a print over the fireplace of the master bedroom. An Early American maple daybed is updated with a faux leopard cushion.

Dark green walls and a four-poster iron bed create a striking guest room. Staffordshire dogs adorn the mantelpiece.

Clements-Gudjonsson Loft
629 Constitution Avenue, NE

Simple and solid, this three-story red brick Colonial Revival building with traditional dentil cornice and keystone lintels was built in 1906 as offices for the Chesapeake & Potomac Telephone Company. In the mid-1980s, it was converted into eighteen lofts.

This building is a good example of the adaptive reuse of an obsolete structure to meet the growing desire for urban housing by young professionals and empty nesters moving from the suburbs to the city. The demand is particularly strong on Capitol Hill because of its stability, vibrant ambiance, and easy access to public transportation. Throughout the Hill, vintage schools, churches, and other commercial buildings like this one, with their impressive architecture and high ceilings, are being transformed into exciting and unique homes.

The dominant design element of the Clements-Gudjonsson loft-style home, with its twenty-foot-high ceilings, is readily apparent: stainless steel. Virtually every surface shines, reflecting light throughout the eleven hundred-square-foot space and making it seem much larger. The owners started out by cladding the wall around the fireplace in stainless steel. Pleased with the results, they kept going . . . and going. Yet to come, ripping out the blond maple floors on the first floor and putting in concrete.

A cable-suspended metal chandelier stacked with bare light bulbs over the dining table give a fragile glow to the hard surfaces.

The large space is divided into two levels. Over the bathroom and kitchen is a long balcony that is used as an office and a bedroom.

Stainless steel appliances surrounded by stainless steel walls, doors, cabinets, and countertops give the kitchen a totally industrial look.

A stainless steel door, prison toilet, and German-made stainless sink used on submarines carry out the metallic theme in the bathroom.

Minimalist black leather furniture includes a sofa by Swiss architect Le Corbusier. On the wall, CDs on rows of rounded metal shelves provide one of the few bursts of color in the apartment.

The living and dining areas are arranged within the twenty-foot-high open space. The 1955 "Number Seven Chair" by Danish designer Arne Jacobsen is used around the dining table.

The bedroom has a steel plate floor with a raised diamond pattern, sliding stainless closet doors, and a ceiling of hand-rubbed silver leaf.

DeLauro-Greenberg House
816 East Capitol Street, NE

It takes a discerning architectural eye to recognize that this house was built in the late twentieth century rather than the late nineteenth. One of three houses designed in the 1990s by architect Eric Colbert to fill a vacant space on fashionable East Capitol Street, it is a spare interpretation of the Hill's classic Queen Anne style. The bones are there with the two-story articulated square bay, arched windows with one-over-one sash, and half-story raised entrance with iron staircase along with a skin of ubiquitous patterned red brick. The house was designed to fit seamlessly into the historic district, not stand apart from it—and does so very successfully.

The interior floor plan is also traditional. A large formal living and adjoining dining room open onto a spacious central hall with a wrap-around staircase rising three stories to the private quarters. Unlike its Victorian-era ancestors, however, the house is filled with abundant natural light from skylights and floor-to-ceiling glass doors that give the rooms a warm, contemporary feel. An extraordinary palette of primary colors provides a vibrant interior that showcases the owners' extensive collection of art and artifacts from around the world.

Retro-inspired art moderne-style furniture is as eye-catching as the artwork. The elephant bowl on the glass coffee table is by artists Dan and Nisha Ferguson, and on the wall to the left is a wooden Moroccan bride's shelf.

Rich-toned walls in the living room are a strong background for the art ranging from a serigraph by Collin Ross, Just For You, *over the fireplace, to a Chinese ancestor portrait on the right.*

Uncle Morty, *a life size papier mâché and mixed media piano player by Deborah Rader, 1999.*

French painter Thuillier's After the Market *dominates the dining room wall above a credenza designed by Robert Mele. Fanciful velvet chairs, originally designed for one of the Beatles, anchor the ends of the table.*

The colors of a striking Turkish rug are echoed in the mosaic surround of the fireplace in the office. Over the glass mantel old fragments of a Sicilian cart are displayed, and on the left side is a ceremonial Turkish robe and headpiece.

The kitchen cabinets are a playful geometric pattern of natural and stained maple. Countertops are inlaid with bands of pure color to complement the woodwork.

In the bathroom, bisazza glass mosaics in concert with Italian ceramic tiles are an homage to Russian Constructivist painter Kandinsky.

Cabinet maker Stefan Alexander handcrafted the master bedroom's furniture as a modern interpretation of the nineteenth-century Biedermeier style, a look the owners fell in love with in Vienna.

The Capitol

No discussion of the majesty of Capitol Hill would be complete without acknowledging the building whose presence gave birth and course to the neighborhood—the Capitol.

The Neoclassical-style structure with its 287-foot-high cast-iron dome, based on Michelangelo's dome for St. Peter's Basilica in Rome, stands in a 131-acre park. The building was meant to impress and inspire, thereby helping to give an identity to the fledgling nation. As the country grew, so did the Capitol. From the time of the laying of its cornerstone by President Washington in 1793 to the present, the building and its grounds have undergone almost continuous alteration and expansion.

As initially conceived by William Thornton, the building was composed of a central structure with a low dome flanked by two rectangular wings. By the time the building was finished in 1826, the growth of Congress required its expansion. The extensions to the north and south with wings and the new dome topped by the statue of Freedom were completed in 1868—more than doubling the size of the building. In the late nineteenth century, the grand terraces surrounding the building were added. No other significant alterations were made until 1962 when expansion of the East Front began. In 2000, ground was broken for an underground visitor center on the East Front that will increase the size of the structure almost 75 percent to 1,355,000 square feet.

Acknowledgments

I am deeply grateful to the generous residents of Capitol Hill—friends and strangers—who graciously opened their homes and enthusiastically supported this project. I am indebted to the Capitol Hill Restoration Society for the use of its archives and wish to acknowledge the work of the Ruth Ann Overbeck Capitol Hill History Project, whose oral history interviews provide valuable information and insights into life on the Hill. A special thanks is also owed to the Stanton Park Neighborhood Association. It is an example of dedication to building a caring community that embraces everyone. And finally, my thanks to Rodger Streitmatter, whose support and patience kept me on track and gave me the confidence to finish.

THOMAS B. GROOMS

For opening their doors to me and my camera, I would like to thank the owners of the homes for making this project possible. I would also like to thank my family and friends. To my parents, Janice and Taylor, for raising me with love and respect, whose nurturing and encouragement made me who I am today. To my brother, Curt, for providing unwavering support and always believing in me. To my sister Felicia and my nephew Bruce, who have been sources of joy and inspiration. To my brother-in-law, Bruce, for his words of encouragement. And finally, to my best friend Kathy for her unending patience, support, and invaluable friendship.

TAYLOR J. LEDNUM

Selected Bibliography

Green, Constance McLaughlin. *Washington Capital City 1879-1950.* Princeton, New Jersey: Princeton University Press, 1963.

———. *Washington Village and Capital 1800-1878.* Princeton, New Jersey: Princeton University Press, 1962.

Herron, Paul. *The Story of Capitol Hill.* New York: Coward-McCann, Inc., 1963.

Metzger, Nancy Pryor. *Brick Walls and Iron Fences.* Washington, D.C.: The Brickyard Press, 1976.

Overbeck, Ruth Ann and Melissa McLoud. "The Building of Residential Washington, 1790-1900." Catalog and exhibit. Washington, D.C.: The Preservation Trust, 1987.

Scott, Pamela and Antoinette J. Lee. *Buildings of the District of Columbia.* New York: Oxford University Press, 1933.

Weeks, Christopher. *American Institute of Architects Guide to the Architecture of Washington, D.C.* Baltimore: The Johns Hopkins University Press, 1994.